Would you believe it!

Grasses

CATHERINE CHAMBERS

Evans

EVANS BROTHERS LIMITED

Evans Brothers Limited
2A Portman Mansions
Chiltern Street
London W1M 1LE

British Library Cataloguing in Publication Data.
A catalogue record for this book is available from the British Library.

Printed by Wing King Tong Co. Ltd., Hong Kong

ISBN 0 237 51541 5

Acknowledgements

Editor: Rachel Cooke
Designer: Neil Sayer
Production: Jenny Mulvanny
Photography: Michael Stannard (pages 28 & 29)
For permission to reproduce the following copyright material, the author and publishers gratefully acknowledge the following:
Cover (top left) Tony Craddock/Science Photo Library, (top right) Robert Harding Picture Library, (bottom left) David Constantine/Panos Pictures, (bottom right) P. Moszynski/The Hutchison Library, (logo insert, front and back) Nick Pavloff/The Image Bank **title page** (logo insert) Nick Pavloff/The Image Bank, (main picture) Sean Sprague/Panos Pictures **page 6** (top) Robert Harding Picture Library, (bottom) Christine Osborne Pictures **page 7** (top) David Constantine/Panos Pictures, (bottom) Mr Jules Cowan/Bruce Coleman Limited **page 8** (top) Tony Craddock/Science Photo Library, (bottom) Felix Greene/The Hutchison Library **page 9** (top) Christine Osborne Pictures, (bottom) Paul McCullagh/Oxford Scientific Films **page 10** (top) Adam Woolfitt/ Robert Harding Picture Library, (bottom) Derek Lomas/Robert Harding Picture Library **page 11** (top) Paul Seheult/Eye Ubiquitous, (bottom) R. Donaldson/Eye Ubiquitous **page 12** (top) Jean-Léo Dugast/Panos Pictures, (bottom) George Bernard/Science Photo Library **page 13** Tony Craddock/Science Photo Library **page 14** (top & bottom) Christine Osborne Pictures **page 15** (top) Lisl Dennis/ The Image Bank, (bottom) Jeremy Hartley/Panos Pictures **page 16** (top) F. J. Jackson/Robert Harding Picture Library, (bottom) L. Foroyce/Eye Ubiquitous **page 17** (top) Barbara Klass/Panos Pictures, (bottom) Nic Dunlop/Panos Pictures **page 18** (top) William Channing/Werner Forman Archive, (bottom) Robert Harding Picture Library **page 19** (top) Bruce Adams/Eye Ubiquitous, (bottom) IMS Photo/Stefan Andersson/Robert Harding Picture Library **page 20** (top) Emma Lee/Life File, (bottom) John Egan/The Hutchison Library **page 21** (top) Sean Sprague/Panos Pictures, (bottom) Neil McAllister/Bruce Coleman Limited **page 22** Christine Osborne Pictures **page 23** (top) Stuart Bebb/Oxford Scientific Films, (bottom) Martyn Chillmaid/Oxford Scientific Films **page 24** (top) Merehurst/The Anthony Blake Photo Library, (bottom) Ronald Sheridan/ Ancient Art & Architecture Collection **page 25** (top) Christine Osborne Pictures, (bottom) Egyptian Museum, Cairo/Werner Forman Archive **page 26** (top) S. Niedorf/The Image Bank, (bottom) John Miles/Eye Ubiquitous **page 27** (top) Christine Osborne Pictures, (bottom) P. Moszynski, The Hutchison Library.

CONTENTS

WHAT IS GRASS?

The green grass that grows in parks is just one of more than 10,000 types of grass. Some grasses are only 2 centimetres tall, others grow up to 30 metres! But they all have roots, stems and leaves like ribbons. And grasses produce flowers and seeds. Rushes and reeds look like grasses, too, but some are not in the grass family.

From baking bread to making umbrellas, people use grasses and rushes in unbelievable ways!

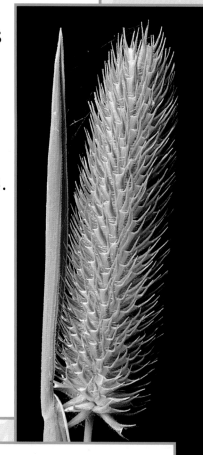

A flowering plant
This is the flower head and ribbon-like leaf of a common grass.

Big bamboo!
Bamboo is a grass. It grows very fast and tall. Its stems are hollow and very strong. In Bali, people have cut this bamboo to build with.

Grass in water

Rice is a grass that grows best in water. The rice we eat is its seeds. It is often grown in flooded fields called paddies.

Rushes and reeds

Bulrushes have long stems, grass-like leaves and thick brown seed-heads. They belong to the sedge family. Their long leaves can be used to thatch roofs.

EATING GRASS

Fresh grasses and dried grasses are eaten by animals. People grind the seeds, or grain, of some grasses into flour. They use this to make bread – or tasty cakes!

Bread
These bread loaves and croissants are made from wheat flour. You can see whole wheat grains on some of the bread.

Crushing corn
In China, maize grain, or corn, is crushed between huge stones to make flour.

The hay harvest
A camel carries dried grass, or hay, in Pakistan. It may be her supper! Hay is farmed as food for many animals.

Sugar cane
Sugar cane is a tall, woody grass. It gives most of the sugar that we use. In Ecuador, people can buy sugar cane from market stalls.

Grass in a Glass

Sweet juice is made from the centre part, or pith, of sugar cane. It is very refreshing. Grass grains are crushed to make oils. Malt made from grain is used to flavour drinks, too.

Making malt
On a malting floor, damp wheat or barley grain is slowly warmed so that the starch in it turns into a sugar called maltose. This malted grain is used to flavour hot milk and other drinks.

Grass perfume!
Citronella grass grows in Sri Lanka. It contains a sweet-smelling oil used to make perfumes.

Oils extracted from corn and wheat are used in cooking.

Rice wine

The Japanese drink a rice wine called saki. It is made from the sticky part of rice known as starch. Starch gives us energy when we eat rice. To make the rice wine, the wet starch is fermented by rotting, until it changes to alcohol.

Juicy grass

In Brazil, you can take your own sugar cane to a roadside juicer. The soft pith is squashed and the juice collected in a bucket for drinking. The juice is also used to make sugar.

GRASS HOUSES

Some grasses can be tough, like wood. They are made into houses, or even bridges. Water rolls easily off some dried grasses and reeds. These are good for making roofs.

Living under grass
A huge dried grass roof, or thatch, covers this house in Vietnam. Grasses and reeds are used as thatch all over the world.

Hollow grass
This bamboo wheel was built over 150 years ago in China to collect water. Its hollow outer rungs filled with water when they dipped into the river. As the wheel turned, the rungs carried the water up and emptied it on to a collecting platform.

Strong grass
In India, bamboo is used as scaffolding. Houses, bridges and water pipes can be made from strong bamboo, too.

SITTING ON GRASS

Some dried grasses are quite stiff, but are often very strong and bendy. People use these grasses to make furniture.

Cutting cane
In Holland, green cane rushes are harvested. The rushes are dried, changing to a pale brown colour, and then used to make cane furniture.

Cane furniture
Lots of different types of dried grasses and rushes are used to make cane furniture. These cane chairs from the Gambia were woven from rushes found growing wild in the River Gambia.

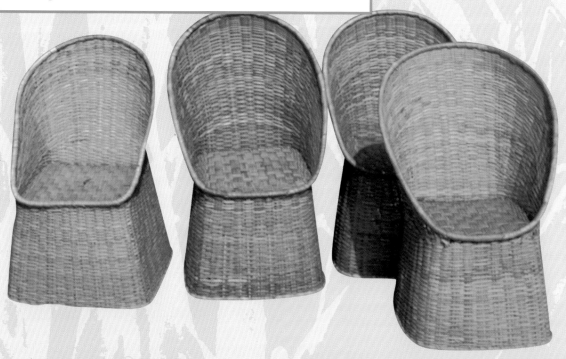

Bendy bamboo!

In Morocco, these chairs are made from bamboo. Large stems are used to make the chair frames. Small stems are split and woven to make seats. Tables, boxes and even beds can be made from bamboo!

Making mats

A woman weaves a patterned grass mat during the dry season in Somalia. You can see that the roof of the house is also made of grass. Stalks of harvested wheat, millet, guinea-corn or maize are used to make mats. Some of the stalks are dyed different colours.

FLOATING GRASS

Bamboo and dried rushes can float.
They have been made into boats
and rafts for thousands of years.

The boats of the gods
In Ancient Egypt, boats were
built from papyrus reeds.
This tomb painting of a reed
boat is 3,000 years old.

Canoe craft
These canoes are made by Uros
Indians on Lake Titicaca in Peru.
A cone-shaped frame of thick reeds is covered with
tall reed stems. In parts of Asia and Africa, round
canoes called coracles are made from woven grasses
covered with animal skins.

Living on a river
Bamboo villages float on a flooded river in Bangladesh. The canes are bent into a half circle to make the houses.

Cane catchers!
In Cambodia, a shrimp catcher is made out of cane. Strips are woven to make a basket. The holes let water through, leaving the shrimps. Bent canes make good handles. Even the pole for lifting the catcher is a cane!

GRASS GARMENTS

Thin, dried grass can be woven or plaited. It makes hats and strong sandals. Soft skirts can be made of grass, too.

Straw socks

Thin dried grass stalks have been sewn into these socks. They were made by Inuits in Greenland, where it is very cold. Grass is light but keeps you warm.

Soft skirts

Grass skirts are famous in the Hawaiian Islands. Long grass is tied to the waist and allowed to hang free. It is not a woven cloth.

Wearing reeds

In Russia, dried reeds are plaited to make a strong material. This is shaped to make hats and boots like the ones in the picture. Ancient Egyptians made shoes from papyrus reeds.

Hats of hay

Straw has been dyed and plaited to make this straw hat. The most famous hats to use fine braided straw like this one are made in Milan in Italy. In Europe 600 years ago, women wore very tall hats with straw baskets stuck on top!

19

BEAUTIFUL GRASSES

Grasses and reeds can be dyed bright colours and bent into strange shapes – sometimes to make pretty bags and baskets, and sometimes just for fun.

Baskets and bags

All types of grass basketware are sold in this Singapore market. Bags, fruit baskets, hanging baskets and fans are beautiful as well as useful.

Delicate dolls

In the Czech Republic, dolls are made from dried, broad maize leaves. The grass basket carries dried flowers.

Plaited wheat stalks are used to make corn dolls in England.

Grass sun shades

Split bamboo makes a strong but light umbrella frame. This is covered with plain cloth and painted. In Thailand, these artists are painting flowers on them.

Colourful fans

Split bamboo is used again to make the ribs for these fans. The colourful silk cloth is attached to these ribs.

21

WARM GRASS

Grass can keep you warm! A heap of dried grass is as good as a blanket. Dried grass also burns well on a fire.

Burning grass
Dried grass is burnt to bake pots and bricks in this kiln in Morocco. It can also be used in bread ovens.

Grass can be heaped over a pile of wood and set alight. The pile slowly burns and turns the wood into charcoal.

Soft and warm

Lambs stay warm on a bed of straw. The air between the straw warms up under their bodies. Bed mattresses can be stuffed with straw, too.

Sweet ripe fruit

Dried grasses are used to pack fruit. It helps stop the fruit from being squashed. Its warmth also helps the fruit to carry on ripening after it is picked.

Straw is laid under strawberry plants for warmth. It also reflects the sun back on to the berries. This helps the fruit to ripen.

PAPER AND PENS

Stiff reeds can be made into pens. Rice grain and the pith from papyrus reeds are used to make paper.

Rice paper flowers

You can't eat these rice-paper flowers! They are made from the stems of the rice plant – not the grain. 'Rice' paper used in cooking is actually made from the pith of a bush grown in Asia.

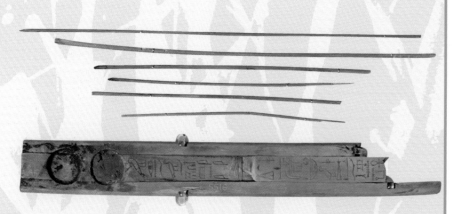

Reed pens

An Egyptian writer used these reed pens and palette nearly 4000 years ago. The pens were dipped in ink held in the palette. Reed pens are still used in the Middle East.

From pith to paper
To make papyrus paper, slices of papyrus pith are soaked and laid down side by side. More slices are put crosswise on top. The layers are then pressed together and dried.

Books of the Dead!
In Ancient Egypt, papyrus Books of the Dead were laid on top of coffins. They told the dead person how to get to the Afterworld. This one shows a woman praying to the hippopotamus goddess, Tauret.

MUSICAL GRASS

A thin reed or piece of grass vibrates when you blow on the edge of it. This can make a note! Hard, hollow grasses can be blown as well – or tapped to give tunes.

Blowing an oboe

The mouthpiece of this oboe is made of two thin strips of cane called reeds. When a player blows on it, the reeds vibrate to make a note. Bassoons and clarinets have reeds, too.

Grass flutes

An Amazon Indian boy plays on his bamboo flute. He blows a thin stream of air across the flute. But the flow of air is broken by a notch cut in the cane. This makes the note.

A grass orchestra!

Huge pieces of hollow bamboo make a good xylophone. Thick bamboo makes different notes from thin bamboo. This orchestra from Bali uses only bamboo instruments.

Piping a tune

Short and long hollow canes make up these Chinese pan pipes. Each length gives a different note. The player blows across the top of each hollow pipe to make the sound.

GRASS CRAFTS

Find out more about grasses for yourself with some art and craft activities. Here are some ideas to start you off.

Growing green hair!

Grow your own grass-haired alien. All you will need are an old pair of tights, a tablespoon of grass seed, a cupful of a mixture of soil and sand (or sawdust), some cotton and buttons and a deep lid from a coffee jar.

• Cut a foot off the tights to a length of about 25 cm.

• Spread the grass seeds in the toe of the tights. Then spoon in your soil mixture, making a ball shape.

• Pinch out a small piece of the tights with the soil mixture in it to make a nose. Wind cotton tightly around its base.

• Sew or stick on button eyes and ears.

• Pour water into the upturned jar lid and carefully place the alien head in it.

• Keep filling up the lid and sprinkling water over the seeds until they sprout. Be patient. This may take a few weeks.

• Don't forget to keep your green-haired alien well-watered and give it a haircut sometimes!

A musical mobile

This mobile clinks peacefully in the breeze or when gently touched. All you need are garden canes of different lengths and thicknesses, coloured string, sticky tape and glue.

• Stick different lengths of string to the canes with sticky tape.

• Wind the end of the strings round the crosswise cane. Stick them down with tape. Make sure the canes are close enough to clink together.

• Tie a piece of string at each end of the crosswise cane to make the hanging loop. Secure each knot with a dab of glue.

Dough shapes

You can't eat the dough used to make these shapes. But you can use it to model toys, badges and ornaments.

You need the following: 250 grams of plain flour, 100 grams of salt, 2 tablespoons of cooking oil, a cup of water and poster paints.

• Mix together the flour and salt.

• Stir in the oil.

• Add the water little by little until you get a soft dough.

• Knead the dough very well, then mould your shapes. If you are making badges, push a safety pin into the back before you bake them.

• Cook the shapes in a very cool oven for about 8 hours or until they are hard.

• Paint your dough shapes after they are baked.

29

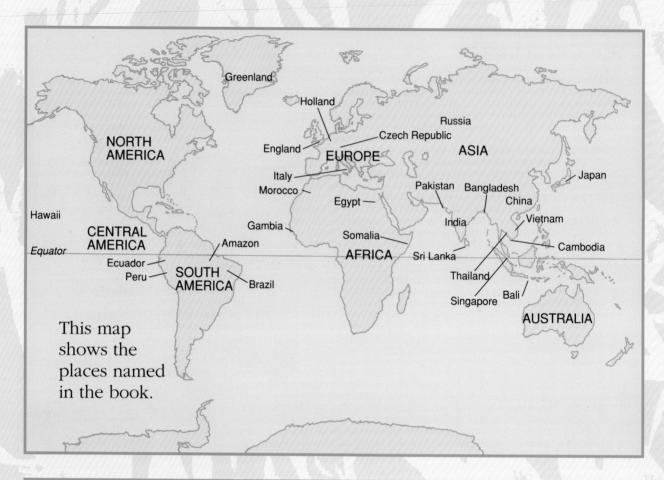

Greenland
Holland
Russia
England — Czech Republic
EUROPE ASIA
Italy
Morocco
Pakistan Bangladesh Japan
Egypt China
India Vietnam
NORTH
AMERICA
Hawaii
CENTRAL
AMERICA
Gambia
Somalia Cambodia
Equator
AFRICA Sri Lanka
Ecuador
Amazon
Thailand
Peru SOUTH
AMERICA Brazil Singapore Bali
AUSTRALIA

This map
shows the
places named
in the book.

INDEX